BLAKE SHELTON

by Jim Gigliotti

Consultant: Starshine Roshell
Music and Entertainment Journalist
Santa Barbara, California

JRVLS
WITHDRAWN
105 3 ST SE
JAMESTOWN ND 58401

BEARPORT
PUBLISHING

New York, New York

Credits

Cover, © Charles Sykes/Invision/AP Photo; 4, © jejim/Shutterstock; 5, © AP Photo/Mark Humphrey; 6, Courtesy Seth Poppel Yearbook Library; 7, © Richard McMillin/Dreamstime; 8, Courtesy Seth Poppel Yearbook Library; 9, © NIK Creative/Alamy Stock; 10, Courtesy SPG; 11, © AP Photo/Chillicothe Gazette/Robert J. Moorhead; 12, © Featureflash/Dreamstime; 13, © Laura Farr/ZUMA Press/Newscom; 14, © Splash News/Alamy Stock; 15, © AF Archive/Alamy Stock Photo; 16, © David Morris/Dreamstime; 17, © Kristin Callahan/ACE/Newscom; 19, © BG017/Bauergriffin.com/MEGA/Newscom; 20, Courtesy Oklahoma Department of Wildlife Conservation; 21, © Derek Storm/Everett Collection/Alamy Stock Photo; 22T, © AF Archive/Alamy Stock Photo; 22B, © Olivier Le Queinec/Dreamstime; 23L, © Isselee/Dreamstime; 23R, © Isselee/Dreamstime.

Publisher: Kenn Goin
Creative Director: Spencer Brinker
Production and Photo Research: Shoreline Publishing Group LLC

Library of Congress Cataloging-in-Publication Data

Names: Gigliotti, Jim, author. | Roshell, Starshine.
Title: Blake Shelton / by Jim Gigliotti ; consultant: Starshine Roshell.
Description: New York, New York : Bearport Publishing, 2019. | Series:
   Amazing Americans: Country music stars | Includes bibliographical
   references and index.
Identifiers: LCCN 2018011084 (print) | LCCN 2018012370 (ebook) |
   ISBN 9781684027286 (ebook) | ISBN 9781684026821 (library)
Subjects: LCSH: Shelton, Blake—Juvenile literature. | Country
   musicians—United States—Biography—Juvenile literature.
Classification: LCC ML3930.S485 (ebook) | LCC ML3930.S485 G54 2019 (print) |
   DDC 782.421642092 [B] —dc23
LC record available at https://lccn.loc.gov/2018011084

Copyright © 2019 Bearport Publishing Company, Inc. All rights reserved. No part of this publication may be reproduced in whole or in part, stored in any retrieval system, or transmitted in any form or by any means, electronic, mechanical, photocopying, recording, or otherwise, without written permission from the publisher.

For more information, write to Bearport Publishing Company, Inc., 45 West 21st Street, Suite 3B, New York, New York 10010. Printed in the United States of America.

10 9 8 7 6 5 4 3 2 1

CONTENTS

A Great Start

In May 2001, Blake Shelton stepped onstage at the Grand Ole Opry in Nashville, Tennessee. At the time, Blake was an unknown. He sang a heartfelt **ballad** called "Austin." Claps and cheers rang out in the concert hall. The crowd loved it! Blake was on his way to becoming a huge country star.

The Grand Ole Opry opened in 1925. It's a place where country musicians perform.

4

Blake Shelton with his guitar in 2001

"Austin" was Blake's first single. For five weeks, it was the number one song on *Billboard* magazine's country music chart.

Outdoor Living

Blake Tollison Shelton was born in Ada, Oklahoma, on June 18, 1976. Blake's dad sold used cars for a living. His mom ran a beauty salon. Blake and his brother and sister spent a lot of time outdoors. "I didn't grow up playing video games," he says. Instead, he caught **minnows** in the creek. Blake loved life in the country.

Blake at age four

Blake enjoyed exploring lakes like this one in Oklahoma.

When Blake was 14, **tragedy** struck. His brother, Richie, was killed in a car accident.

Getting Started

Growing up, Blake dreamed of being a country music singer. He started singing when he was just a boy. At age 12, he learned to play the guitar. When he was 16, Blake performed at a local club. After high school, Blake moved to Nashville—the center of country music!

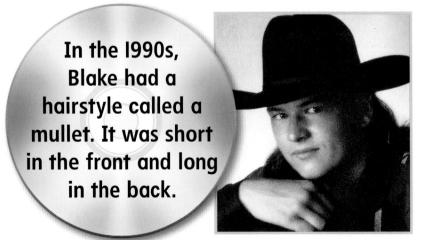

In the 1990s, Blake had a hairstyle called a mullet. It was short in the front and long in the back.

Nashville is home to many country music clubs.

Hard Work

In Nashville, Blake did not become a star right away. However, he never gave up on his dream. Blake wrote songs and sang whenever he could. He also worked as a painter and a mover to earn extra money. It would take eight long years before "Austin" became a hit single. The song's success eventually led to Blake's first album in 2001.

Blake's first album cover

Blake performing in Nashville as a young singer

Blake's **debut** album, *Blake Shelton*, reached number three on the country music charts.

Remembering Richie

Blake had finally become famous. His songs "The Baby" in 2003 and "Some Beach" in 2006 reached the top of the charts! In 2005, Blake met country singer Miranda Lambert. They fell in love and got married in 2011. Together, they wrote a song about Richie, Blake's brother who had died. It was called "Over You."

Blake and Miranda Lambert

12

"Over You" was named the Country Music Association's (CMA) 2012 Song of the Year.

TV Star

In 2011, Blake became a coach on the TV show *The Voice*. He remembers his own long road to success, which makes him a great coach. Even as a TV star, Blake continued to top the charts. He was named the CMA's Entertainer of the Year in 2012. In 2014, he was CMA's Male **Vocalist** of the Year —for the fifth year in a row!

Blake with his 2014 CMA award

Blake sits in his judge's chair on *The Voice*.

Blake's singers have won top awards on *The Voice*.

JRVLS
105 3 ST SE
ESTOWN ND 58401

Hit After Hit

In 2013, Blake released *Based on a True Story . . .* The CMA named it Album of the Year. Five of its songs became number one singles. In 2017, Blake released yet another album, *Texoma Shore*. Each of Blake's 11 albums have been big hits!

Blake named *Texoma Shore* after Lake Texoma, which is on the border of Texas and Oklahoma.

Blake signs an autograph for a fan.

A New Style

Blake is known for more than his hit albums. He has helped create a **unique** style of country music. Some people call it "bro-country." It includes **aspects** of rap, hip-hop, and electronic music. Other bro-country artists include Jason Aldean and Luke Bryan.

Blake has had 25 singles reach number one on *Billboard*'s list.

Blake sings with his band on the *Jimmy Kimmel Live* TV show in 2017.

True to His Roots

Blake is a huge music and TV star. However, he still lives in Oklahoma. "Unless it's raining, I'm hunting or fishing or farming," he says. He is one country star who never left his down-home country roots.

Blake holds a huge paddlefish he caught in an Oklahoma lake.

On Halloween 2017, Blake was a guest on *The Today Show*. Co-host Hoda Kotb (right) dressed up as Blake!

Blake has more than 20 million followers on Twitter!

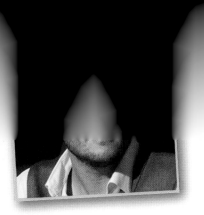

Here are some key dates in Blake Shelton's life.

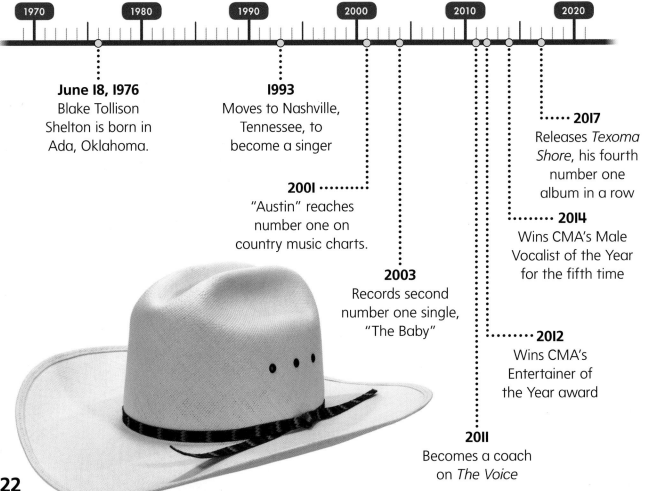

1970   1980   1990   2000   2010   2020

June 18, 1976
Blake Tollison Shelton is born in Ada, Oklahoma.

1993
Moves to Nashville, Tennessee, to become a singer

2001
"Austin" reaches number one on country music charts.

2003
Records second number one single, "The Baby"

2017
Releases *Texoma Shore*, his fourth number one album in a row

2014
Wins CMA's Male Vocalist of the Year for the fifth time

2012
Wins CMA's Entertainer of the Year award

2011
Becomes a coach on *The Voice*

22

Glossary

aspects (ASS-pekts) particular parts or features of something

ballad (BAL-uhd) a song or poem that tells a story

debut (day-BYOO) the first public appearance of something

minnows (MIN-ohs) types of small freshwater fish

tragedy (TRAJ-uh-dee) a sad and terrible event

unique (yoo-NEEK) unlike any other

vocalist (VO-kah-list) a singer

Index

Read More

Tieck, Sarah. Blake Shelton: Country Music Star (Big Buddy Bios). Minneapolis, MN: ABDO (2013).

Tometich, Annabelle. Today's Hottest Music Superstars (Today's Superstars). Minneapolis, MN: Lucent Books (2016).

Learn More Online

To learn more about Blake Shelton, visit
www.bearportpublishing.com/AmazingAmericans

About the Author

Jim Gigliotti is a former editor at the
National Football League. He now writes books
on a variety of topics for young readers.